The Art of
FRANK HOWELL

Yellow Bead

The Art of
FRANK HOWELL

TEXT BY MICHAEL FRENCH

DOUBLEDAY

Published by Doubleday
a division of
BANTAM DOUBLEDAY DELL PUBLISHING GROUP, INC.
1540 Broadway
New York, New York 10036

Doubleday and the portrayal of an anchor with a dolphin are trademarks of Doubleday,
a division of Bantam Doubleday Dell Publishing Group, Inc.

Cataloging-in-Publication Data is available from the Library of Congress.
ISBN: 0-385-32234-8

The text of this book is set in 15-point Adobe Granjon.
Book design by Susan Clark Dominguez
Manufactured in the United States of America
October 1997
BVG 10 9 8 7 6 5 4 3 2 1

When one stands before any kind of art,
it should tell nothing.
It should, however, create the infinity
of questions begetting questions.
It should be a mirror that is not superficial,
in that it reflects the physical self.
That reflection is emotional and historical
but it is a pathway to insight
into a more spiritually significant present.

—*Frank Howell*

Frank Howell and his son, Frank

To all my children, but especially to Heather and Frank.
They are my teachers and bring to my life all that I truly need.

The Art of
FRANK HOWELL

Every year the art of Frank Howell becomes known to an expanding body of collectors, national and international gallery patrons and, through his illustrations of the poetry of Nancy Wood, readers inspired by the powerful spiritual faith of American Indians. Howell, who has Lakota Sioux bloodlines, is variously described by critics and collectors as a symbolist, a mystic, a spiritualist and an existentialist. The interpretation of the forces of time and nature, significant themes in Howell's art, touches on all those roles. The wind that flows through an old man's hair or caresses a wisp of smoke is a metaphor for the passage of time and the connectedness of all things. Movement is energy, and energy is life. Studying Howell's figures, we become aware of the relationship between past and future, the shift in perception that can turn us from child to wise elder and back to child again.

To talk with Frank Howell is to find both the child and the elder. He is charming and soft-spoken, with an outward calm that disguises an ever-churning energy within. When he is overworked or has to deviate from a schedule, he can show flashes of impatience, but mostly he is rock steady. He has the burly frame of a boxer—he pursued boxing, along with wrestling, for many years—and, at age fifty-nine, he is still graceful and athletic. His face has the cast of a careful observer. He is fond of quoting Picasso's dictum, "Let me always see as a child," and indeed, there is something of the innocent in Howell. With deeper levels of meaning, he continues to draw some of the same images that fascinated him as a boy. A pair of hands, a bird in flight, the face of an old man or woman. He can look upon the familiar and see something no one else sees, be filled with wonder or passion, and through his painting reveal to us his sense of discovery.

The message Howell likes to communicate is about our place in the universe and, whether we acknowledge it or not, our responsibility to all life-forms. In many ways Howell is a private man, possessive of his time, but he will share his feelings and philosophy with almost anyone who promises to listen sincerely. He considers this his role as a teacher, which is as important to him as being an artist. Words come

Flowers

easily as his eyes glide over everything around him, picking up details, but he chooses his sentences carefully. It becomes clear that his philosophy is not one of platitudes but was born of his growth as a person and an artist.

Despite the archetypal depictions of American Indians for which many admirers know him, Howell is sensitive to being called an American Indian artist. Rather, he sees himself as an artist who happens to be an American Indian. The distinction is important to a man who has had a strong dislike of labels since childhood. "Once you're put in the box of being an American Indian artist—put in any box, really— that's what people expect you to paint," he says. "It's what you become. People who should know better can't seem to see you any other way."

Howell can and does paint landscapes, still lifes and figure studies, but preconceptions and misconceptions are difficult to overcome. He says, "The general viewer believes that what an artist is currently painting is what he is, that he has arrived at what he does because of some acquired belief system and that is how he will think and what he will do the rest of his artistic career. However, this is not true of me. If I am not growing, I am dying." With every new work, he challenges himself technically or with different subject matter. "These changes," he says, "are never revolutionary, but evolutionary. They are quiet and subtle and may go unnoticed by most, but they are there and important. Too much attention is paid to a presumed subject matter while the real content, which is profound, is overlooked."

He has an equivalent objection to gallery patrons who look at a painting's price, its title and the signature of the artist before seriously studying the painting. Just as he insists on observing the world around him with a child's fresh eyes, Howell asks the same honest, direct attention of anyone encountering his art.

His versatility with subject matter and genres notwithstanding, Howell will admit that American Indians, and the Lakota Sioux in particular, spur his strongest passions. The Sioux were the fiercest of all Plains tribes, fighting to the death in virtually every battle, and the last to make peace with the United States government. It is not by coincidence that Crazy Horse, Red Cloud and Sitting Bull, three of our most fabled American Indian warriors, were all Sioux. Their spirit has not been lost on Howell, who embodies the same fierce independence. But the Lakotas were also craftspeople, poets, mythmakers and seers. The true vitality of a culture lies not in its armies but in its artists. In the late nineteenth century, the Sioux were the backbone of the Ghost Dance Cult, a mystical effort to unite all American Indians and restore the power that the white man had usurped, not by guns but by spiritual renewal.

Throughout Howell's drawings, sculpture, paintings and mixed-media works, there is a poetry in the lyrically detailed lines of an Indian's flowing hair, the feathers around his neck or the ceremonial mask he wears. Howell's often solitary characters inhabit a physically spare but spiritually rich universe that is haunting and even surreal. Their faces are unusually old, weathered, androgynous, and they hint of secrets and insights. It doesn't matter that many of the faces are neither clearly male nor female. In Howell's eyes, spirituality transcends gender.

In some works we find ravens perched on a figure's head or shoulders, as if a link to another world or time. The raven is a symbol of bravery and uncanny intelligence to many American Indians, as well as to people in other cultures. This and other favorite symbols—feathers, hummingbirds, smoke and wind—give Howell's work a mystical dimension, lifting it from the literal to the metaphoric. They evoke the spiritual attributes of a people who have known oppression and survived it with a dignity and resoluteness that teach us not just about American Indians but also about the human condition.

The cover of this book, Howell's well-known *Circle of Life,* evokes for us the dignity and wisdom of the survivor. The imagery in this richly textured acrylic painting is universal. The central figure, a shaman wrapped in his red blanket, is in

Night Chorus

Winter Gathering

a pose of contemplation or evocation of the forces of life. His large, expressive hands seem to be telling a story, represented in the subdued but richly detailed petroglyphs that surround him. We find people, birds, plants, pregnant animals—all connected in the same matrix, the same circle. Birth is at the beginning of the circle, and death is at the end, but it is a circle that continues indefinitely.

In American Indian belief systems, as in those of other cultures, when we die we fulfill our purpose, and someone takes our place. The petroglyphs in the painting symbolize not only life and regeneration but myth in its classic definition—a legendary narrative that expresses the beliefs of a culture. Without myth, Howell believes, a people cannot survive or understand its place in history. However, when too many subcultures—from street gangs to political factions—create their own myths, the fragmentation of a culture begins. These myths are bogus, he says, if they are ignorant of universal truths. As much as anything, perhaps, *Circle of Life*—and indeed all of Howell's work—is about the importance of recognizing and honoring the universal in our daily lives.

Circle of Life

Circle of Life

"On the canyon wall behind the shaman are the etched images that represent part of the history of the lives, the land and the spirituality of his ancestors. They speak to us, from many centuries past, of the physical and spiritual connection and interdependence of all things. Family members to family members, people and animals to the land, birth to death, and many other representations of the circle of life are addressed. The shaman reflects on the gifts of the past and the importance of passing on those ideas and values for the future of his people."

Night Echoes

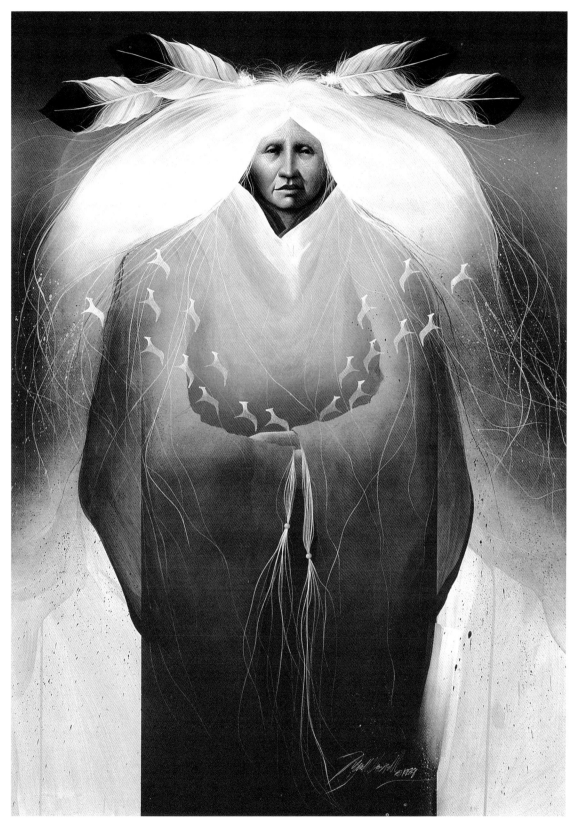

Ember

Raven

"Despite angry winters, wildflowers grow. Despite the never-ending night, there is still a light. The grandfather's light . . . a hand to a path for tomorrows."

Raven

Harvest Dancer

Harvest Dancer

"The sad and timeless warrior still walks the dry prairie clay. The winds of winter are gone, and there are no hungry cries from his children."

Wounded Knee Woman

"A shield is not necessarily used to ward off projectiles launched by enemies. It is also used to invoke spiritual powers to intervene on the behalf of the creators. The shield can also contain references to actual events, past or present, to which attention needs to be drawn or which require some action. It can be a warning, as in this multimedia piece. The warning tells others of the loss of loved ones, stolen land and the storm of white settlers and soldiers covering the homeland."

Wounded Knee Woman

Pecos Storm

Pecos Storm

"North of Pecos, New Mexico, the ranchland is fed by melting snow, and spring and summer rainstorms. After a storm, the clouds and magnificent wet land glow in crystal-clear air."

Spring Matrix

"The garden is within. The matrix, the womb of harmony is within. Beneath the distraction of discordant voices, noises, and misdirection is the self. Listen: A new spring is possible."

Spring Matrix

Lakota Woman

Lakota Woman

"The young Lakota woman wears a dress decorated with many elks' teeth. The dress has great power and meaning. It is a gift from her mate, who is a warrior and accomplished hunter."

Blue Estuary

"October winds whistle through branches and bent grass. Now and then a small voice rides along."

Blue Estuary

White Hummingbird

"The White Hummingbird was once a wise and giving woman of the ancient ones who became the Lakota people. She now flies into the living world to teach a worthy one the path of love and understanding toward all things. She will teach of gentleness and sharing with all people. She is sent to teach of goodness and knowledge of the past. She must teach the woman she finds, who will become the new messenger, to be wise in all those things and aware of all the people to come in the future. Only then will her mission be complete. She will kiss the chosen one, and she will not fly again."

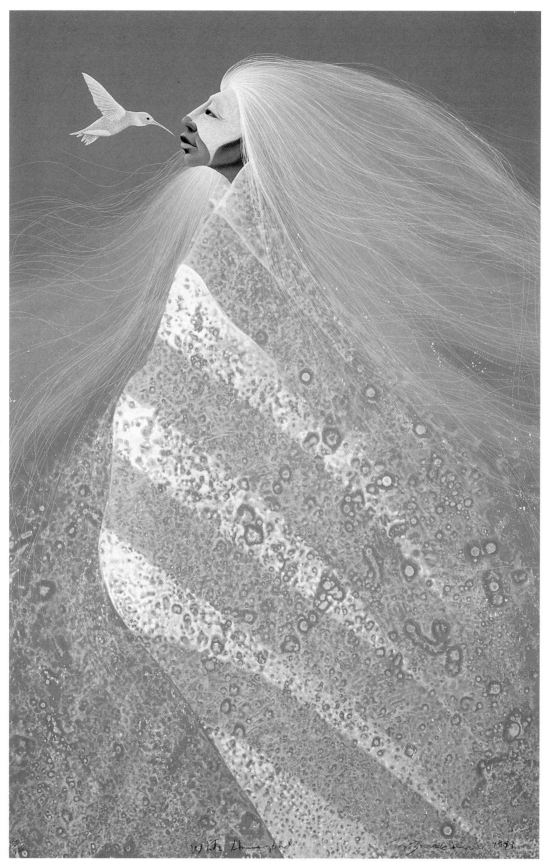

White Hummingbird

Turquoise Earring

"The elderly wise man, a shaman, lives alone in the Southwestern mountains. He is seen rarely, but when he appears it is to speak of something that has come to him in his solitude. When his soft voice is heard, everything around him grows silent. His gift to his people must be understood."

Turquoise Earring

Born on July 31, 1937, in Sioux City, Iowa, Frank Howell was the only son of a U.S. Army Air Force enlisted man who was one quarter Lakota Sioux. His mother was English and Irish American. Howell's childhood was full of charged and contradictory emotions. The unpredictability of military life took the family from Sioux City to El Paso, Texas, and back to Sioux City before Howell turned seven. In the next ten years, the demands of helping to raise his two younger sisters and refereeing the frequent arguments between his parents forced on Howell a caregiving role he was not old enough to assimilate.

It was not surprising, then, when he played a far different role in school, dictated by his impressive physical presence and a need to stand out. What he needed most was a life of his own, one without so much responsibility. The occasional prank got him noticed; many more made his reputation. Soon he was the subject of continuing reprimands; but he continued to flout authority. Howell got his first label: rebellious and largely unteachable.

The serenity and spirituality inspired by his American Indian figures fail to hint at the slow and arduous process that led Howell personally to that harmony. In the roiling sea of home and school, his one safe harbor was his paternal grandmother, a half Lakota Sioux named Mary Mike, who lived nearby. In his grandmother's modest home, Howell found a refuge that wakened his senses and his intellect. There was almost always the smell of baking bread, music on an old Victrola, a continually replenished pile of books and magazines brought home from the Salvation Army, where his grandmother worked. Mary Mike taught her grandson to crochet, to sew, to cook and to sing. Unlike anyone at school or at home, she saw his talent and nurtured it. There was always movement in her house, things changing, things becoming. She stressed to her grandson the importance of the senses, particularly the sense of touch; she emphasized that no piece of craft was ever finished until the artist could touch and even caress it, absorbing and validating the energy within.

Among the books Mary Mike brought home were illustrated medical texts, depicting both human anatomy and medicinal plants. She might have hoped that her grandson would become a doctor. Instead, intrigued by the intricately detailed illustrations, Howell set out to draw and paint them. With long evenings and weekends to copy bones and muscles and exotic plants, he began his lifelong habit of delving almost obsessively into his subject matter, sometimes endlessly painting and repainting the same object, never quite considering it finished. He was guided by a sensitivity to detail and a desire to draw or paint an object as it had never been seen before.

Howell says that even at this age he was "awed and transformed by the thought of being an artist," seeing art as a kind of magic because of its transforming powers. Such powers must have appealed on a deeper level to a boy whose daily life was hardly ideal. To escape through the window of art must also have helped unleash his imagination. But he was enough of a realist to know that being an artist also meant discipline and sweat. While Howell was certainly born with artistic abilities, he knows that without a work ethic, his career would never have been born.

Howell's deep interest not only in the final product but in the process of art, in the intellectual and emotional journey that defines creativity, was also inspired by his grandmother. In Lakota culture, the importance of patiently sitting and observing and listening, of developing one's intuition, was the basis for understanding the universe and one's relationship to it. Besides the rich music and conversation at his grandmother's house, there were equally long periods of silence as Howell pursued his craft of sewing or drawing, all the time letting his senses absorb everything around him. The Lakota universe was one of magic and myth, of phenomena felt more than explained. Besides copying and recopying images in the medical books,

Braids

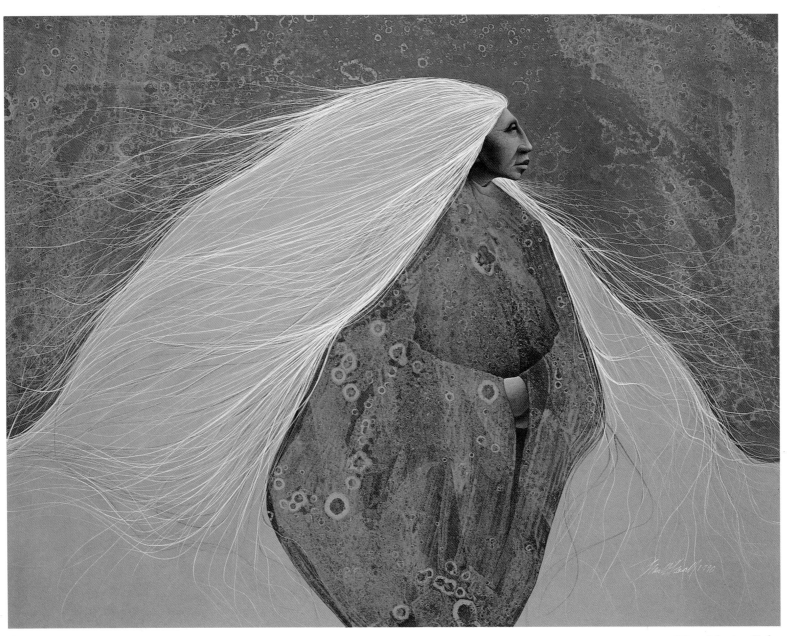

New Mexico Echo

Howell would draw hummingbirds metamorphosing from flowers, and hands turning into feathers or clouds. Any image was possible if one had the intuition to see it and the discipline and skills to bring it to life.

Around age fourteen, Howell began to think of art as a serious calling, though he kept it a secret from almost everyone. At church one Sunday he listened as the minister, citing the life of Job, exhorted anyone in the congregation who had talents to share them, especially with those who were less fortunate. The earnest young artist felt a stirring of altruism. He could paint and draw virtually anything, couldn't he? He could help others by sharing the talents God had given him. Only when the minister finished speaking and the collection plates began to circulate did Howell recall that in the Old Testament *talents* referred to a denomination of money. The minister had been imploring his congregation to tithe. Embarrassed, Howell resolved to keep his self-proclaimed calling more private than ever. But he was also convinced that his interpretation of the sermon was not totally wrong, and that the seed of teaching and helping others had been firmly planted in him.

Through his adolescence, the nurturing lessons Howell learned from his grandmother continued to be at odds with the chaos of his home and school life. His mother had never completely approved of his spending time at Mary Mike's, or with his paternal great-grandmother, who lived farther away but who was another source of storytelling. The thought of her husband's and son's communicating with that half of the family made Betty Howell angry and resentful. The result always seemed to be a loud argument between her and Frank's father, while Frank lost himself in countless drawings.

Besides his mother's frequently voiced anger and insecurity, Frank Howell had to contend with another kind of doubt, this one from his father. Marion Howell didn't talk much about his family and heritage, for fear of provoking his wife. Like many urban American Indians of his generation, he didn't talk much about bloodlines.

Prejudice was something to ignore or hide from rather than fight. So rare were prideful discussions about family or the "old" ways that for many years Frank Howell was not sure what or whom to believe about his family. What little family history was transmitted he learned from his grandmother.

The mixed messages the young Howell received only sparked questions about his own identity. The easiest answer was to believe that the messages didn't matter, or at least to act that way. His years of defying authority culminated on the eve of his high-school graduation, when Howell commandeered a twenty-ton steamroller and drove it hell-bent through downtown Sioux City. The police finally pulled him over and arrested him.

Except for his grandmother, by now Howell had exhausted the patience of almost everyone who knew him. A judge suggested that in lieu of jail the defiant truant consider joining the U.S. Marine Corps. Howell took the judge's advice.

For the next three years, duty with the marines offered Howell an outward discipline to complement the structured intuition he had learned at Mary Mike's. For the first time he was taking charge of his life, and if he wanted to prove himself, which he did, the marines' high standards were clear and specific. Off duty, he continued to pursue physical challenges wherever he found them—motorcycle and car racing, judo, wrestling—and often recklessly.

His willingness to put himself in harm's way may have reflected his still unresolved anger, but the artist in him also understood that only when he was consciously facing danger were his perceptions and feelings truly crystallized, his appreciation of life the greatest. Risk and danger were also a means of confronting and overcoming his fears. Howell has always believed in testing his limits. Artists who largely repeat themselves on every canvas, he says, have stopped taking risks and therefore stopped growing. With maturity, Howell's infatuation with physical danger diminished. But his willingness to challenge himself emotionally and

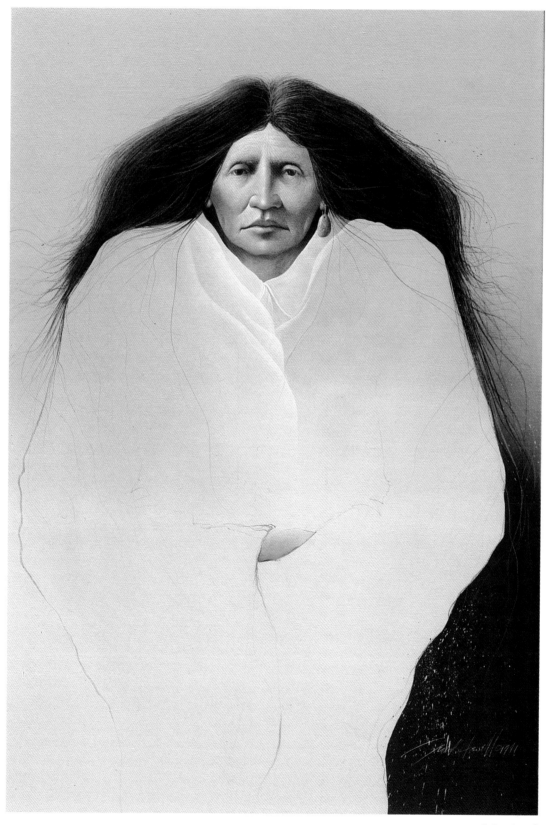

Matriarch

White Buffalo Woman

intellectually, his tendency to gravitate more to questions than to answers, became a lifelong characteristic. And it complemented the intensity and curiosity of this man who demanded both change and perfection in his work.

In 1958, honorably discharged from the marines, Howell enrolled in the University of Northern Iowa and, later, the University of Iowa Writers' Workshop. For the next six years, as he got married, earned his undergraduate degree and later taught graduate courses, he was still reluctant to declare openly his love for painting. In the Midwest, it was easier to gain respect for one's baseball or wrestling skills than it was for a sketch of a tree. Worse for Howell, abstract expressionism was the rage in the late fifties, from the toniest New York art circles to the smallest Midwestern campus. Howell, a naturalist and realist to his core, wanted nothing to do with the abstract movement or the art classes it inspired at the university. He was given permission, through independent study, to develop his drafting, drawing and painting skills with minimal assistance from faculty. His relative isolation might have bothered other young artists, but the largely self-taught Howell found it productive and satisfying.

Well disciplined after the marines, and more determined than ever to prove himself, Howell capitalized on an unusual personal asset. In the marines he had found that he could virtually give up sleep, existing on as little as two or three hours a night, and still remain alert and focused. While he had always found mornings his most productive period, in college he stayed up till all hours, painting anything and everything, tolerating all distractions. He overwhelmed his teachers with both his productivity and his proficiency. Howell was so determined to learn on his own rather than trust someone else's opinion that the first time he tried painting with egg tempera, he used the white of the egg instead of the yolk. Someone soon pointed out his error, but Howell was not one to be intimidated by his mistakes. He continued experimenting with every facet of his craft and was indifferent to negative responses.

For an artist, he knew early on, the specter of fear or doubt was the most dangerous threat to creativity.

Despite his outward confidence, within a year of finishing school Howell began a period of intense self-questioning. He had, by choice, never been close to Iowa's mainstream art community, but without the structure and support of the university he felt suddenly adrift. Where was his art taking him? What was he trying to say? Did he really have a worthwhile message? Maybe he was too prolific. The self-doubts began to create troubling bouts of artistic paralysis, and after a while he grew dissatisfied with almost everything he painted. One night he stopped working altogether. It was as if, Howell says, he had entered a fog and couldn't find a beacon of light anywhere. His normally reliable intuition had shut down, and just as uncharacteristically, he was listless and tired.

During this crisis of confidence, Howell attended an exhibit of paintings by Mauricio Lasansky, the head of the University of Iowa's art department, at the Des Moines Art Center. Lasansky's work, titled "Nazi Drawings," riveted Howell as nothing before had. The powerful renderings of war atrocities left the young artist so spellbound that he insisted on camping out in front of the drawings well after the center's closing hour. For the first time in his life, Howell says, he understood "the ability of art to render an emotion." Art was suddenly more than colors or anatomical exactness or a movement with a label—it was pure, unadulterated power. Howell's mission in life was reconfirmed. He would create images that would reveal so clearly what he was feeling that anyone seeing his art would feel the same as the artist.

Cactus Flowers

Fire Ponies

Lakota Wings

Desert Sunset

"Everything we have known of this land where my father and his father's father lived is gone. The animals that fed and clothed our people no longer roam the prairie. We no longer roam the prairie. Long fences stretching from the east divide our land. The sun is setting on our people and on what is now, for us, an empty desert."

Desert Sunset

Grandmother's Gift of Fire

Grandmother's Gift of Fire

"Grandmother, your hands, your face recalled, still warm the lonely child."

Emergence (diptych)

Emergence

"The sense of an omnipotent power able to influence the direction of all experiences and events, including life and death, prevailed on the lives of both believers and nonbelievers. Various vestiges, fetishes, songs and words were used to atone for unacceptable acts or to invoke the omnipotence to respond favorably to the requests of a petitioner. The belief that the power of the light, the omnipotent force to be reckoned with, was from above, created prayers and reaching hands, directed toward the heavens, in search of redemption."

The Sweetgrass Women

The Sweetgrass Women

"Alone, together, they wait, each with her own memories, joys and sorrows, each with her own images wrapped in fear. Where are the men? There is gunfire in the distance. Are they alive? Will they return? The women share a silence that drowns all other noise."

Sarah Begay

"Sarah Begay never saw her beautiful daughter or the Navajo land that was her home. Blind from birth, she had never seen anything with her eyes. Since I met her and her daughter at a trading post near Chinle, Arizona, I have never forgotten her. When I painted her, I wanted her to have eyes."

Sarah Begay

Songs for Questions

Songs for Questions

"The night wind is a river, a swift and steady current of memories and questions, stirring the sediment of yesterdays."

She-Rain
Summer Prophecy

"As told in the messages from the old ones, a gentle rain, a She-Rain, will slowly nourish the hungry earth. When it is time, when she is needed, she will come to keep the people and the land strong."

She-Rain Summer Prophecy

Pecos Autumn

"West of the Pecos River, the landscape is beautifully diverse. In the semiarid high desert, the usually subtle, grayed colors of autumn explode after rain or an early snow."

Fruit from the Light

"The omnipotent light from above touches the fertile earth, and life begins."

Fruit from the Light

Howell now approached his art with renewed energy and purpose. He was determined that his work would communicate emotion directly to the viewer. But that was easier said than done. What exactly his feelings were, Howell was not sure. The intellectual currents in which he swam during this period continually challenged his perceptions of the world. He became immersed in psychology, particularly the writings of Carl Jung and the Swiss psychiatrist's idea of the collective unconscious. Joseph Campbell's theory, dovetailing with Jung's, of archetypal myths and the role of the hero throughout history in all cultures also intrigued him. So did the pivotal metaphor in Hermann Hesse's *Siddharta* of the timeless river that represented both consistency and change. Nineteenth- and twentieth-century Russian novelists such as Dostoyevsky and Pasternak supported Howell's Lakota belief in a universe of conflict and struggle but also of miracles and mystical intervention. The Hegelian dialectic of thesis, antithesis and synthesis also played in his mind. He absorbed all these powerful and intertwining concepts into his canon of personal beliefs. The challenge was to find the right visual metaphors to express them.

By now Howell was teaching high school in a small community in Iowa, and he spent several summers teaching under the auspices of the federal Office of Economic Opportunity in a program called Upward Bound. The program was designed to challenge bright and talented but underachieving high-school students. Howell was selected to team-teach in a communications course that involved arts and crafts, poetry and prose, and civics. No doubt Howell saw himself in many of his students, and he plunged into the task of "sharing his talents" with such energy and sincerity that he had little creativity left over for his own painting. As his output dwindled, his response was to push himself even harder. Working most of the night again, he was determined to assimilate into his art the concepts he had been studying. The results were maddeningly disappointing. What was the voice inside really telling him? If he had a vision, why couldn't he articulate it on canvas?

Frustrated, he began to question whether he was really an artist. It was one thing to have technical skills, another to express something deeper. As his doubts spiraled inward, he found himself unable to function even as a teacher. His marriage began to deteriorate. He lived, he says, in an ever-deepening silence. The paralysis was similar to the one he had experienced after college, but now there was no one to intercede or inspire him. Howell saw no alternative but to commit himself to a nearby psychiatric institution for an evaluation.

After a battery of interviews and tests, the doctors informed their patient that he was a paranoid schizophrenic. Howell admitted that he had strong and conflicting emotions, and he was looking for help. But he wasn't crazy. He was an artist. No one accepted his explanation. He was informed that he could not be released without successful therapy. He was stunned. The doctors refused to tell him how long he would be held against his will or what his therapy would involve.

Howell likened the next three and a half months to the plot of Ken Kesey's *One Flew Over the Cuckoo's Nest*. Medicated with liberal doses of Thorazine, he was shunted from psychiatrist to psychiatrist, therapy group to therapy group. Everyone poked and prodded at his psyche. At last a young doctor from India, with an outsider's fresh view of the Midwest, suggested what Howell must have already sensed. The young artist didn't belong in Iowa. Howell took a moment to grasp the words that would mean more than his physical liberation. "You're an artist. Follow your instincts. Work through your problems with your intuition. Don't listen to others. And get out of town." After collaborating with the doctor on specific coping strategies, Howell was released. Within a week, he had separated from his wife, packed his bags and left Iowa.

Howell jumped to Detroit and the rejuvenating powers of a major city. To support himself, once again he took up teaching, this time at an all-black inner-city high school. As an art instructor, he patiently extended himself to those who didn't

Symphony II

Bouquet

repeated applications were interspersed with a thin varnish until the final rich, smooth tonality resembled that of an oil painting.

A similar effect was achieved in *Canyon Echoes,* another later work whose technical genesis lay in Colorado. Here Howell experimented by adding alcohol to his acrylic paint to achieve luminosity. With the same egg tempera technique mastered by Crivelli, but using acrylics, Howell relied on extremely fine lines and cross-hatchings to create the linear contours of the face and body. Employing a layering process that involved as many as forty applications of glazes, adding highlights and shadows along the way, he created the mass and depth necessary to give the work its vitality.

To create the highly distinctive hair in *Lakota Blue Aura* and in his other paintings, Howell stands at a slight distance from the canvas and paints not just with his wrist but also with his arm and shoulder. Using a No. 1 brush with its extremely fine point, he will "pull" a strand of hair by moving his entire body across the surface from one side of the canvas to the other. This is a technique he first mastered as a commercial sign painter. By slightly spinning or rocking his wrist as his body moves along the canvas, he controls the amount of paint released by the brush in a reverse capillary action. The line of the hair becomes finer as it becomes longer—and Howell has painted them as much as eight feet long—as he gradually and imperceptibly pulls the brush off the canvas, until the line ends in an almost microscopic point. With extreme patience, he paints each hair one at a time.

Now a succesful artist, Howell hoped to reconcile with his parents, and at his invitation they moved to Breckenridge. In spite of everyone's best intentions, what followed was a disaster. Howell felt helpless and overwhelmed. His parents ended up liking Breckenridge and staying. Howell, accepting that some conflicts can never be resolved, moved on with sadness.

An April Voice

Atira's Grace

Grandmother's Echoes

"In the warmth of a sunset, memories whisper of Grandmother. Her gentle face appears, then quickly disappears . . . a brief but beautiful gift."

Grandmother's Echoes

Deer Dancer

"The spirits of deer rise above the dancers. Lives are taken because of the need to survive, but it is not without understanding, gratitude and honor. The native peoples know that any being is as they are themselves. In the struggle for survival, when any being made by the Great Spirit loses the fight, he is no less or greater than those who live on. He has taken his place in the great circle of life. A birth is a path of the circle, and the end of life fulfills one's purpose in the greater circle."

Deer Dancer

Elk Dreamer

Elk Dreamer

"The visions of the Elk Dreamer were sought after in times of great hunger or sickness. The great elk, a powerful and healthy animal, was more meaningful to the native people than just a source of food or hides. Elks were followed and watched by healers to find the grasses, leaves and herbs that they ate. It was thought that these were the medicines to heal and make the ill strong again."

Warrior's Song

Warrior's Song

"The warrior seeks guidance through visions. Visions can come in many ways, but the seeker must be pure of purpose so that he will be visited in a good way."

Visitor

"Darkness comes, and White Face Woman appears in the eastern night sky. She rises above the hills beyond the Lakota camp and smiles a bright smile."

Visitor

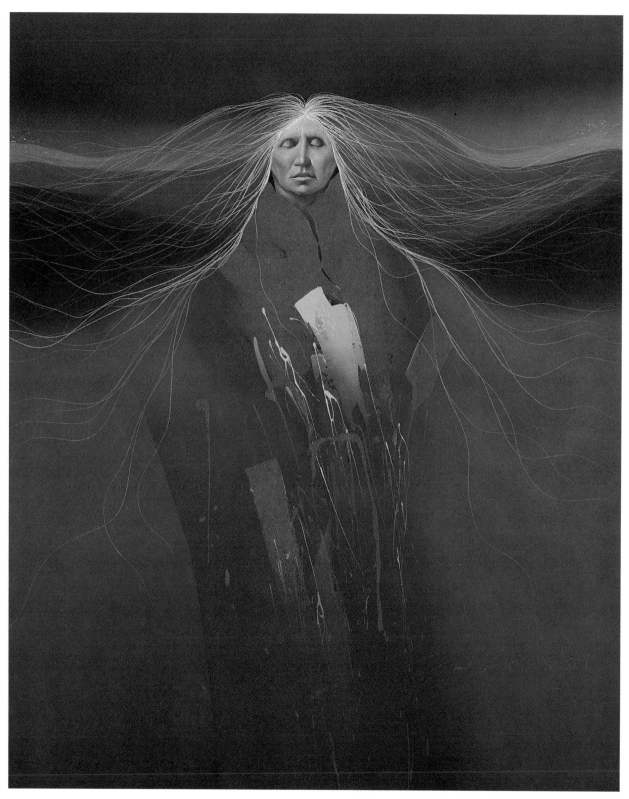

Southwest Sunrise

Southwest Sunrise

"A sunrise caresses the land and its native people. It is a new dawn, a new beginning, within the life-giving light."

The Encirclement of Sisters

"Between heaven and earth all things are flowers, blessings to experience, beauty for enriching our lives. As the physical and spiritual relationship of all peoples is ultimately and irrevocably symbiotic, if we are to survive, so it is between us and all the other creatures and things of our world."

About three hundred miles south of Breckenridge and seventy miles north of Santa Fe lay Taos, tucked into the tailbone of the Rockies. Except for some impressive mountains, the Taos landscape was quintessential northern New Mexico and substantially different from Breckenridge. Here the rolling, almost hypnotic piñon-covered hills, Pueblo-style adobe homes as pink as the earth, and tableaux of Taos street life struck a chord in Howell. While living in Colorado he had visited Taos several times, and he was no stranger to the galleries that lined its historic plaza. He had painted some Taos scenes, and they had sold well. He also felt comfortable there from a business standpoint. Like Breckenridge, Taos was small, and its economy was largely dependent on visitors, many of whom liked buying art that depicted the picturesque town.

Howell settled into the former house and studio of Leon Gaspard, an oil painter who, along with another Russian immigrant and artist, Nicolai Fechin, took a permanent liking to northern New Mexico. Howell shared their reaction, drawn intuitively, he says, to the area's "rocks and caves and bones, to its hidden places." In love, as well, with the light and intimate charm of the Gaspard studio, he eventually bought the property from the artist's widow and entered one of the more important periods of his artistic life.

Howell began his stay in Taos by painting more landscapes. Along with other artists of the early seventies, he helped evolve a genre known as contemporary Southwest—vignettes of mountains, gorges, cacti, adobe homes—which, like his Colorado landscapes, proved immensely popular with collectors. But while his contemporary scenes made him a comfortable living, Howell was making a breakthrough on a more serious front. Working in his studio one afternoon, listening to music—something he had done habitually while painting since college—he experienced a revelation. It was as if, he says, all his technical skills, spiritual growth and understanding of philosophy finally merged, and the images he was starting to paint on simple Masonite board transcended everything he had done before.

Fire Songs

Using graphite pencil, watercolors, and powdered graphite, alone or in combination, he created a gallery of faces that he calls Amerinds—spirits out of the neolithic past. On a very superficial level they resemble American Indian elders, but metaphorically we sense much more. Their hair is swept and molded by the wind—the "breath of God" to many American Indians—rooting them in the present but also transporting them to the next destination. Their hands or arms arc skyward in an incantatory gesture. Their faces are serene, heads half bowed, eyes half closed, delivering a message that is intuited rather than articulated. Implicit in their wraithlike appearance is the knowledge of dreadful secrets, but just the fact that they appear for us is a sign of hope and renewal. They bring the sacred to our mundane lives. They might even be viewed as characters in a mystery play, voices of wisdom that, while muted, evoke responses in us.

The music that started Howell on this journey was not merely incidental to the images he drew. Howell had always appreciated classical music, but for the first time, he was truly *hearing* the music, his senses tuned in to an undercurrent that clarified his own internal energies. Perhaps those energies were the anger and doubt he had pushed deep inside him, or the guilt over his failure to solve the problems of people he was close to—heretofore negative forces that now could be shaped into the vision he had been struggling toward.

In the next six months Howell produced twenty-five drawings that, although separately titled, together formed what Taos gallery owner and critic Lawrence Kaplan called "an orchestral mosaic." The collection, known as "Past Winds," represented, in Kaplan's words, the mystery of creativity, and "the artist as visionary . . . a servant of forces too complex and mighty for him to understand other than dimly." In other words, Howell played the role of shaman, a magician who could conjure up the past or the unconscious in all its wonderful, terrible power.

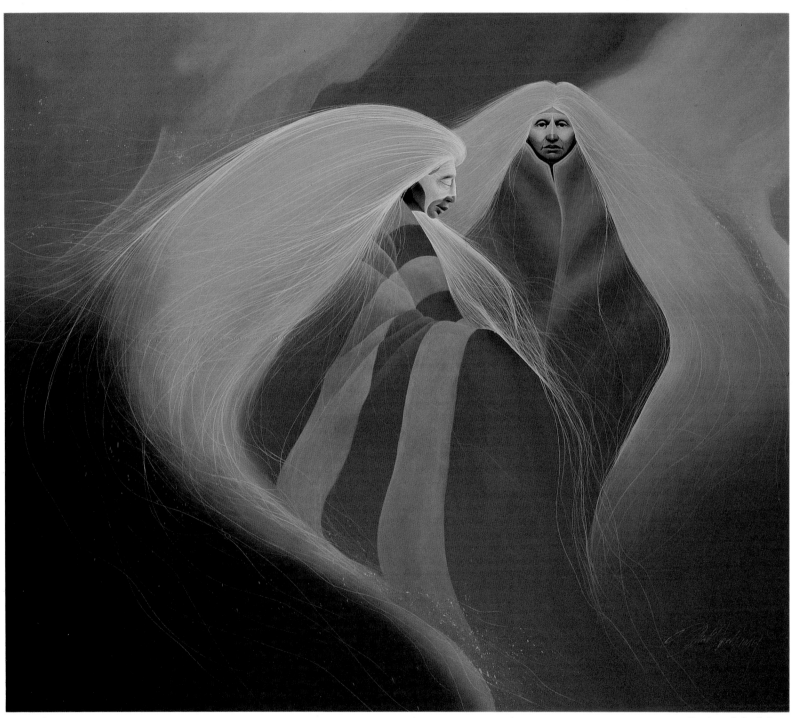

Paths of the Moon

These drawings expressed Howell's ability to grasp the intangible, his willingness to take risks and keep asking questions of himself. The faces rendered in "Past Winds" are now familiar to those who know Howell's work, but at the time they represented a significant departure for an artist principally recognized for landscapes and figure studies. Years earlier, on one of his first trips to Taos, Howell met the poet Nancy Wood. They collaborated on *Many Winters,* and the book's illustrations of Taos Pueblo life strengthened Howell's reputation for finely rendered portraits. The American Indian figures were meant to be purely representational, confirming Howell's skill with lines and light and shadow. His subsequent collaborations with Wood, however, *Spirit Walker* and *Dancing Moons,* clearly owe their origins to "Past Winds," as docs much of his current work. In "Past Winds" we are asked to see beyond the immediate. Howell's dreamlike imagery offers a sense of movement, of things becoming and transforming. In a world of magic and metamorphosis, we feel part of the transition, a voyage that both excites and frightens us as it takes us into the unknown.

As productive as were his two years in Taos, Howell began to grow impatient with small-town life. He was permanently in love with the expansive vistas and earthy colors of northern New Mexico, but Taos itself felt confining. His art was now attracting a national audience, and he was busy traveling to keep commitments. In 1975 he moved to the Cherry Hills area of Denver, though he promised himself that he would one day return to New Mexico.

For the next ten years, Howell both broadened his technical skills and experimented with subject matter, challenging himself to go deeper into the world of unconscious myths. Sometimes he painted conventional American Indian portraits, but more often his faces became metaphorical. The half-lidded eyes took on a Buddha-like aura. The hair grew long and fine and transformed itself into feathers or flowers. The lines that suggested a neck or shoulder became fewer and bolder and added tension.

His nights were spent reading, revisiting favorite authors like Hesse and Campbell and discovering the Greek philosophers. Aristotle's and Plato's aesthetic philosophies dealing with the complicated interrelationship of art and music and poetry intrigued Howell. Experimenting, he played with elemental images, trying to reduce art, as Plato urged, to its most basic form: the simplest lines, the purest colors, the strongest emotions. Howell believed that poetry, perhaps the most distilled of the art forms, could be translated to canvas.

Howell also read everything he could on the religion and culture of prehistoric societies, using his new insights to push himself as an artist. One revelation was that many of the beliefs and symbols of the American Indian were also found in other cultures and religions, particularly Buddhism. The circle of life, for example, with birth and death viewed as processes rather than as ends, was readily understood by both Buddhists and American Indians. Both also believed in teaching responsibility. There is a Buddhist metaphor that all humanity climbs a ladder, and just as someone on the rung above has a duty to reach back and pull us to the next level, we have a duty to help those on the rung below. American Indians, relying on an oral tradition, used countless myths and metaphors—from stories of coyotes to ones about gods to those concerning war heroes—to stress the necessity of interdependence in preserving the community. One of Howell's laments about modern culture is that interest in lessons of the past has been eclipsed by technology and fascination with the future.

Howell was also devoting much of his protean energy to business. He opened several galleries, showcasing both his own art and that of other painters he admired, as well as a lithography shop in a basement below his studio. He had first learned the art of drawing on stone during a trip to Milwaukee several years earlier. With typical

Summer Berries

Summer Dance

determination, he honed his skills as a lithographer, and in Denver acquired a reputation that attracted almost more business than he could handle. He was a pioneer in moving away from the use of heavy, cumbersome stones and temperamental aluminum plates to random-grained Mylar. It was easier to correct mistakes on Mylar, a medium that provided the same finished product as conventional stone or plate lithography but was less expensive and more portable.

As in his Breckenridge days, along with being an artist and running his businesses, Howell continually made himself available to civic and philanthropic groups. The downside of having unusual reserves of energy was that he took on too many projects, only to be overwhelmed with obligations. By the end of his decade in Denver, his time was no longer his own. He knew he was in trouble, he says, when he had to buy a second tuxedo. The desire to teach and extend himself to others, along with the drive of a man who had grown up poor and wanted to prove himself, fought with his need to be left alone to create. In 1986, in an effort to retrench and consolidate, Howell left Denver for Santa Fe. The return to the spiritual landscapes of northern New Mexico was a conscious effort to choose the role of creator above all others.

Pale Rose

April Transcendence

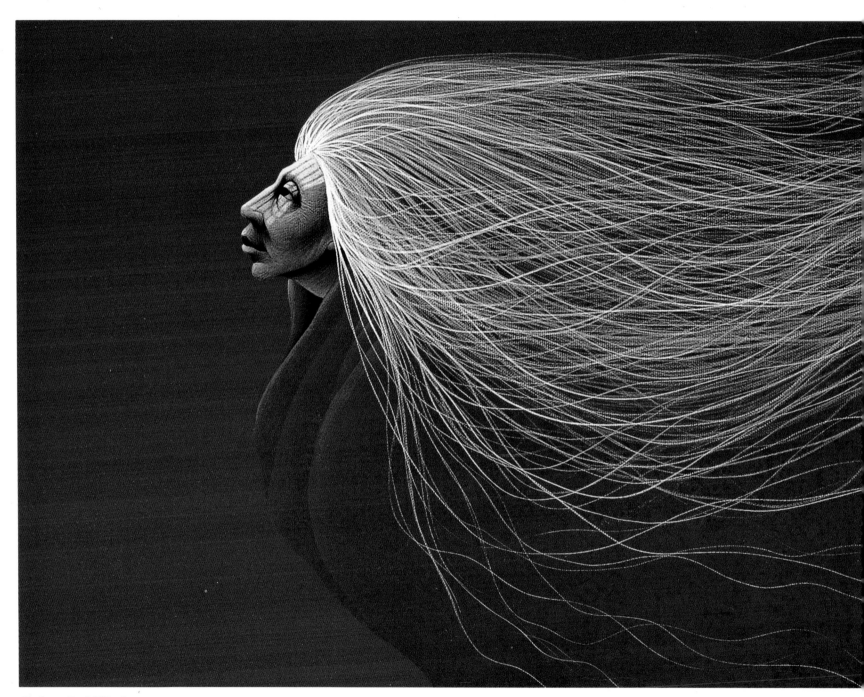

Dakota Red Wind

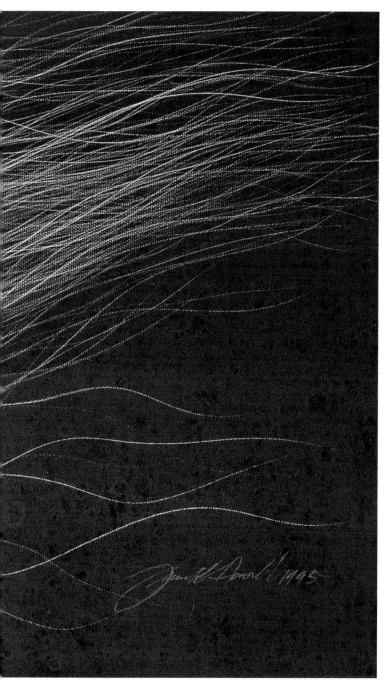

Dakota Red Wind

Dakota Red Wind

"Angry and sorrowful winds blow in the hearts of the Lakota. This land, which the white intruders claim as theirs, is no longer for the people to freely camp or hunt in. Everyone is hungry and without hope. A great fight is coming."

Sky Sentinels

"Ravens are messengers and sentinels for Plains people. Because they are honored and respected, they watch for enemies and warn of potential danger."

The old woman walked to the center of the village, sat down and closed her eyes and did not speak. Twice the sun rose and went down again but still she did not speak — the third night she began to sing beautiful songs — Prayers — Beautiful prayers for safety for her people. The following morning she opened her eyes — and in a circle around her were twelve black stones. She rose and went to each stone — picking them up and kissing them. She sat in the center of them and began to sing again. The stones began to Flutter and turned to Ravens. As one of the ravens moved toward her, she stopped singing. The Raven spoke — Amongst with prayers and songs and Wherever your people go — we will be there — Sentinels in the sky

Sky Sentinels

Metamorphosis Red Cloud

Metamorphosis Red Cloud

"In his vision the warrior saw a great war chief who was carried away into a setting sun. Once the chief was there, fiery colors swirled around him and his people. Churning red clouds entered his head and body, and the sky turned black. When he emerged from his spirit journey, he understood the path he must follow. He knew he must use the fire in his heart, the power he had been given. He knew he would be called to lead his people."

Winter's Bride

Winter's Bride

"The pale woman appeared at the edge of the camp. As she stood in falling snow, she motioned to a very old man struggling to reach her. 'It is time,' she said, 'to be with me again. The long winter calls. You have lived a long and brave life and I have missed you.'"

Crow Messenger

Crow Messenger

"The crow or raven messengers mediate between the living and those in the other world. They bring word of love, concern and hope of being reunited. The blue-black creatures were often honored by songs and prayers, and used as personal adornment. They were stuffed with many items that were thought to be powerful medicine. Sometimes they were wrapped with a red cloth or rawhide and attached to hair or garments."

Spirit Shield

"The spirit shield speaks of harmony, of balance and a quiet heart: to see clearly for oneself and for the benefit of others. To lead a life filled with learning, to strive for a harmonious spirit, enables one to become a profound teacher."

Spirit Shield

Black Moon

Black Moon

"Memories like leaves and stones pile one upon the other. Layers, too numerous to count, become the sediment to sift in the river of the night."

The Cloud Dreamer

"At the edge of wind, out of the darkness of beginnings, rising from the womb of Mother Earth, promises that were only promises begin to flower under the fertile sun."

The Cloud Dreamer

Grandfather's Echoes

"When captive warriors and leaders of the Plains Indians' resistance were jailed or confined to camps, they were given ledger paper so that they could make drawings and paintings that were traditionally done on hides. These works became known as ledger drawings. The drawings were done from memory or from stories of brave deeds in battle and other events of their past. They are valued for both their artistic and historical significance. The background of this painting is a replication of one of these drawings, and in the foreground is a relative of the creator."

Grandfather's Echoes

With his return to New Mexico, Frank Howell began a period of remarkable productivity. For the past eleven years, besides his art, Howell has found time to pursue photography, giclée printing (Iris ink printing), more reading and time with his family. He has learned to delegate rather than consume himself with details, including running another gallery, this one on the corner of Santa Fe's historic plaza. While he continues to challenge himself artistically, he is at a point that allows him to take a well-deserved breath or two.

Howell's phantomlike Amerinds, the neolithic spirits he created during his Taos period, have yielded in Santa Fe to images of shamans, seers, and wise elders—people, like the artist who creates them, at peace with themselves. Part of his reverence for the elderly no doubt springs from his youthful relationship with his grandmother and great-grandmother. But he also believes that enlightenment comes only with time and experience.

In *Reunion,* Howell's most recent work as of this writing, we see an older woman in traditional Sioux dress, surrounded by hummingbirds in flight. The birds are all different—male, female, large, small, some gloriously colored, while others have almost monotone feathers. They are industrious, energetic, quiet, full of mystery. In Howell's vision, hummingbirds are reincarnates, bringing messages of love or hope or just a sense of connection. The woman who summons them with such concentration may be doing so out of personal need or respect and love for the dead. It is hard to read her expression, an ambiguity that gives the large acrylic a necessary tension. We sense that her abilities are unusual, a gift bestowed only on those with the purest heart or clearest mind. The reincarnates who visit are eternal denizens of the collective unconscious, and perhaps even guides to the afterlife.

As with most of his work, the idea for *Reunion* came, Howell says, not from any specific individual or incident but from his imagination. He describes his best ideas as "spontaneous snapshots of the subconscious." They might just as well be called

Reunion

brainstorms, because Howell says his imagination can, at any time, be overwhelmed by a specific physical image. If the image is also emotionally compelling, he will put it on canvas. Much can go wrong, however, between the preliminary glow of inception and the afterglow of completion. An artist's drawing skills, composition and sense of color have to be disciplined and executed flawlessly.

For *Reunion,* that meant first covering the canvas with a coat of pale green acrylic, lightly sanding it, then adding a second coat. Once the canvas was dry, he flooded it with a deeper green shaded with reds and blacks, blotting it with paper towels to create texture. This work had to be done quickly to achieve a consistent effect. Howell applied a thin, transparent glaze, on top of which he added more green for even greater depth and texture.

To create the hummingbirds, Howell cut out paper templates and placed them around the woman, experimenting to determine which placement gave the greatest sense of movement and energy. The actual painting of the birds, like the woman's dress and beadwork, required his characteristically fine brushstrokes. Obviously, such work is exacting and time-consuming.

Howell's colors are also precisely thought out. Although he once experimented with almost pastel tones, relying on subtle gradations in color, he now likes bold, deep and resonant hues, often primary colors, to give his work balance and energy.

No doubt Howell would describe his own energy as one of his most valuable assets. It is the thread that links his artistic periods, along with the view that art, like life, is a process. He is inclined to revisit old paintings and themes with new eyes, a new sensibility, a new spiritual being. The moment he stops growing and learning, Howell predicts with a twinkle in his deep-set eyes, he will stop creating. Until that unlikely time, he will keep making windows through which others can view a special universe, which this contemporary shaman evokes with clarity and passion.

Reunion (detail)

Reunion

"Words left unsaid, words needing to be repeated and words longing to be heard come from the other world on whispering wings. With them they bring messages and warnings, and sometimes a touch, for the relatives who call them with long-ing and love."

Trading Post

Dream Keeper

Elk Horn and Herbs

"The Elk Dreamer seeks visions for understanding the powers of the elk, a blessing given to the people by the Great Spirit. The elk has mystical knowledge of herbs and medicines found in mountain forests."

Elk Horn and Herbs

Wounded Knee Winter

Wounded Knee Winter

"The spirits of the fallen rise above their bodies. The cries of anger and fear are no longer heard. There is no more pain. There are no more questions."

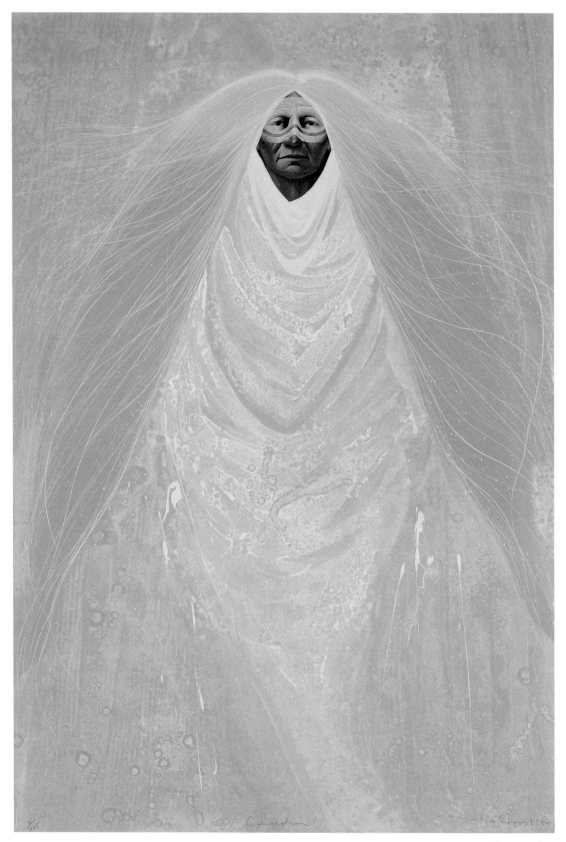

Conception

Sunrise Garden

Past Winds—Fugue of the Mystery Force

Past Winds—Fugue of the Mystery Force

"The ancient ones open their mouths, and the beginnings of music echo across the land. Songs, lessons for tomorrows, emerge and must be sung to the people and to the Great Spirit."

Silent Whispers

"Many things between people are understood without words. Eyes are closed when kissing or embracing another to see more deeply. Often silence is better for a journey through the heart."

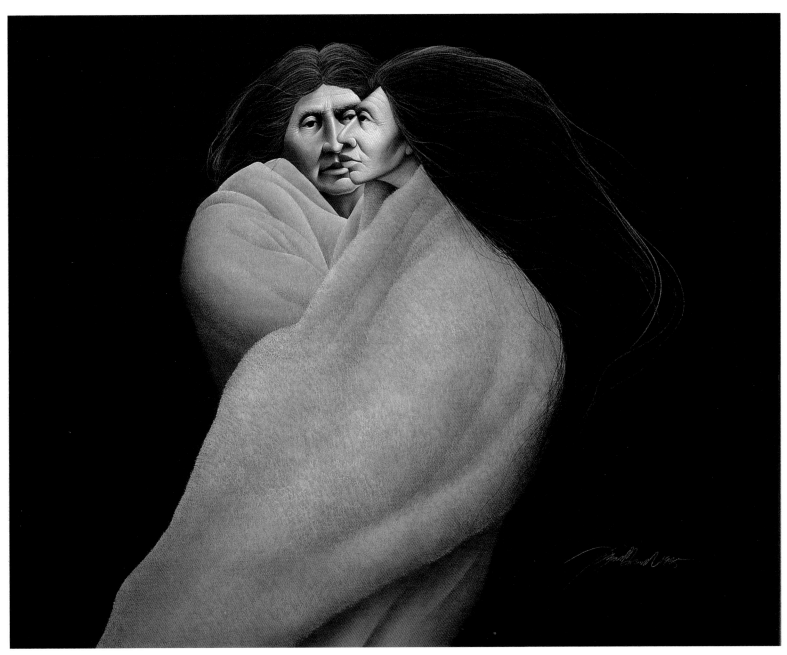

Silent Whispers

Brulé Reunion

Brulé Reunion

"The warrior watches and listens with closed eyes. Voices of the grandfathers arrive on wings from their other world."

Spring Cloud

"April clouds float above a Dakota prairie. Memories, too, of other springs come and go, adrift on the winds from yesterday's storms."

Spring Cloud

Night Garden

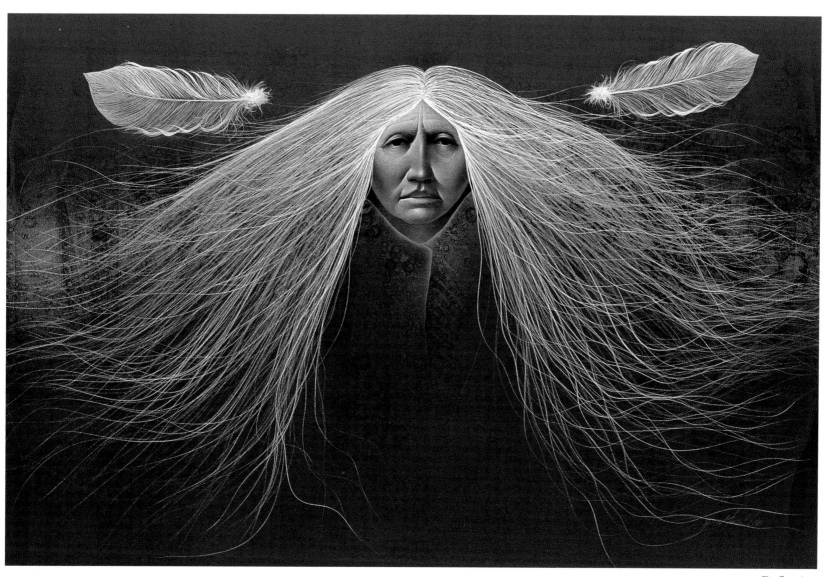

Reflection

Blue Raven

"What is this obsession, this thing called art: this mistress who steals one's heart and ultimately one's life? What, in its introspective yet manic passion, does this demanding lifelong affair produce that is so satisfying, so addictive? After a few successes and so many failures, what is it that drives an artist to come back to face, fight and caress another blank sheet of paper or canvas? Where, and to what purpose, is all this effort leading?

"These questions have been asked by every creative person who has ever written, painted, sculpted, photographed, danced or made music. Every individual may not arrive at definitive answers, but each recognizes and understands the questions, and that is enough. The right questions finally lead to understanding. Understanding brings wisdom and, with it, recognition of the need for more profoundly constructed questions. This is the childlike, inquisitive mind of the creative soul, which sees and questions like an intrigued and awed child. This is learning, and learning creates the desire for more learning.

"There are few days off, and no retirement, from this entanglement of knowledge, passion and vision that will be molded and converted into creative expression. There are no guarantees of acceptance, understanding or reward, but the noise inside the mind never ceases. I will paint today, tonight and for as many tomorrows as I am given. What I paint doesn't matter as much as *that* I paint. The joy of the journey is in the learning through doing."

—*Frank Howell*

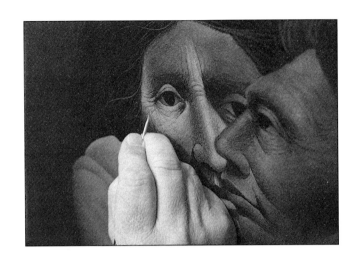

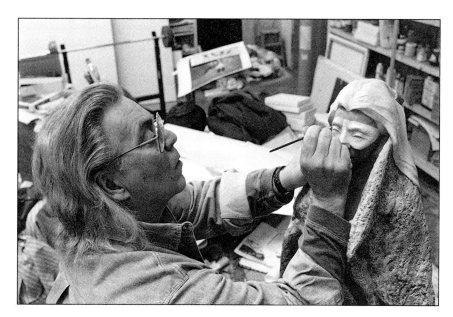

Index to Paintings